FROM EGG TO SPIDER

Anita Ganeri

Heinemann Library
Chicago, Illinois

© 2006 Heinemann Library
a division of Reed Elsevier Inc.
Chicago, Illinois

Customer Service 888-454-2279
Visit our website at www.heinemannraintree.com

Designed by Ron Kamen and edesign
Printed and bound in China by South China Printing Company

10 09 08 07 06
10 9 8 7 6 5 4 3 2 1

Library of Congress Cataloging-in-Publication Data
Ganeri, Anita, 1961-
   From egg to spider / Anita Ganeri.
      p. cm. -- (How living things grow)
   Includes bibliographical references.   ISBN 1-4034-7860-0 (library binding - hardcover) -- ISBN 1-4034-7869-4 (pbk.)
   1. Spiders--Life cycles--Juvenile literature. 2. Spiders--Eggs--Juvenile literature. I. Title. II. Series.
   QL458.4.G36 2006
   595.4'4--dc22
                              2005026924

Acknowledgments
The author and publishers are grateful to the following for permission to reproduce copyright material: Alamy pp. 7, 15,
21; Ardea pp. 14 (Bob Gibbons), 19 (Steve Hopkin), 29 (Steve Hopkin); Corbis pp. 6 (Steve Austin/Papilio), 13 (Tim
Zurowski), 26, 27; FLPA pp. 8, 18 (Jef Meul/Foto Natura); Holt Studios p. 25; naturepl.com pp. 4 (Bernard Castelein), 5
(Lynn M. Stone), 16 (Geoff Dore), 17 (Geoff Dore), 22 (Premaphotos), 23 (Premaphotos); NHPA pp. 9 (Laurie Campbell),
11 (N A Callow), 20 (George Bernard), 24 (Stephen Dalton); Photolibrary.com p. 12; SPL p. 10.

Cover photograph of a spider reproduced with permission of Getty Images/Iconica/Steve Satushek.

Illustrations by Martin Sanders.

The publishers would like to thank Lawrence Bee for his assistance in the preparation of this book.

Every effort has been made to contact copyright holders of any material reproduced in this book. Any omissions will be
rectified in subsequent printings if notice is given to the publisher.

The paper used to print this book comes from sustainable resources.

Some words are shown in bold, **like this**. You can find out
what they mean by looking in the glossary.

Contents

Have You Ever Seen a Spider?

A spider is an animal with four pairs of legs. There are many kinds of spiders. Spiders live all over the world.

*Most spiders make **silk webs**.*

The garden spider lives on plants in gardens and woods.

You are going to learn about a garden spider. You will learn how a garden spider is born, grows up, has babies, gets old, and dies. This is the spider's life cycle.

How does the spider's life cycle start?

5

Spider Eggs

The spider starts life as a tiny egg.
A **female** spider lays the egg. In the
fall, the female's body is large and
full of eggs.

The female spider spins a little bag from **silk**. This bag is called an **egg sac**. She lays over 800 eggs inside the egg sac. Then, she closes the sac with more silk.

The female spider fixes the eggs sac to a plant or under a window.

Who looks after the eggs?

Guarding the Eggs

Hungry birds and **insects** eat spider eggs. Frogs sometimes eat spider eggs, too. So, the spider looks after her eggs.

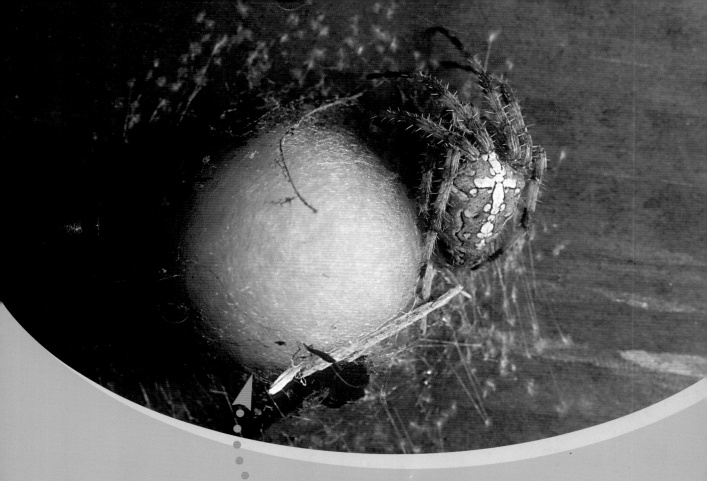

*The **female** spider sits close to the **egg sac**.*

She does not leave the eggs. She does not even go looking for food. She guards the eggs until she dies.

When do the eggs **hatch**?

9

The Eggs Hatch

Inside each egg there is a baby spider. During the winter, the spider eggs start to **hatch**. But the baby spiders do not leave the **egg sac**. They are safer in the egg sac.

At first, the baby spiders stay in a tight group like this.

The baby spiders grow bigger. When spring comes, they bite little holes in the egg sac. Then, they crawl out.

What is a baby spider called?

Baby Spiders

The baby spider is called a **spiderling**.
She is pale yellow. The spiderling stays
close to the other spiderlings.

*The spiderlings look like
a wriggling **swarm**.*

But the spiderling is in danger!
She will be lucky to live. Birds eat
many of the spiderlings. Some are
even eaten by other
spiderlings.   Do the spiderlings
                                 stay together?   13

A Balloon Flight

A few days later, the **spiderling swarm** splits up. The spiderlings start to live on their own. The spiderling has a wonderful way of finding a new home.

These spiderlings on lines of silk wait for a breeze.

14

The spiderling spins a long **silk** thread. Then, she waits for the breeze to blow it away. This is called **ballooning**. The spiderling's new home is where she lands.

Spinning a Web

In the early summer, the young spiderling spins her **web**. The spiderling makes **silk** in her body. She uses the silk to spin her web. She spins it in a bush or between two plant **stems**.

Every day, the spiderling mends any gaps in her web. Then, she sits in the middle of her web. She waits for something to eat.

What does the spiderling eat?

Sticky Trap

The spiderling eats **insects** such as butterflies, flies, and wasps. She waits for an insect to fly into her **web**. The insect gets trapped in the sticky web.

The spiderling takes the insect to the middle of her web to eat it.

The spiderling rushes to the insect. She wraps it up in **silk**. Then, she kills it with a bite from her **poisonous fangs**.

How fast does the spiderling grow? 19

Growing Bigger

The **spiderling** grows bigger. Her skin gets too tight. It splits along the sides. She wriggles out of her skin. This is called **molting**.

Just like this spider, a garden spider's new skin is soft, but it dries hard.

Under the old skin, the spiderling has a new and stretchy skin. She changes her skin about five times. Then, she is fully grown and is called a spider.

Time to Mate

In the early fall, the **female** spider is ready to **mate**. A **male** spider waits by her **web**. He gently taps on the **silk**.

The male spider has to be careful. The female might think he is food!

The male garden spider is much smaller than the female.

Then, the male and female spiders mate. In the fall, the female spins an **egg sac**. She lays her eggs in it. The next spring, these eggs will **hatch** into **spiderlings**.

When does a spider die?

23

Spider Lives

Adult spiders might **mate** many times. After mating for the last time, the **male** spider has done his job. He dies.

The adult **female** spider lays her eggs in the fall. The spider life cycle starts again. After the female has laid her eggs, she dies.

Where do spiders go in the winter?

Winter Chill

Winter is a hard time for a spider. The weather is cold. There is not enough food to eat. The adult garden spiders die before the winter. Only their eggs **survive** until the next spring.

The spiders that **hatched** this year find a warm place. They live through the winter. These spiders will **mate** next year. The **females** will lay more eggs next fall.

26

Life Cycle of a Spider

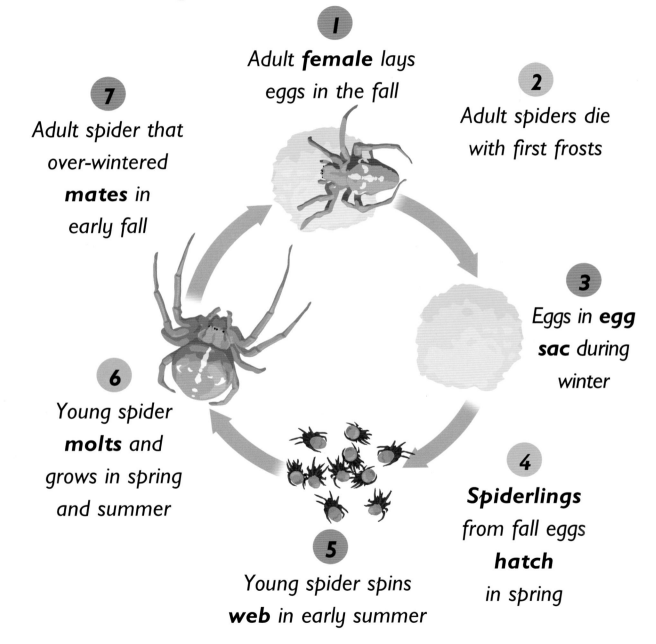

1 Adult **female** lays eggs in the fall

2 Adult spiders die with first frosts

3 Eggs in **egg sac** during winter

4 **Spiderlings** from fall eggs **hatch** in spring

5 Young spider spins **web** in early summer

6 Young spider **molts** and grows in spring and summer

7 Adult spider that over-wintered **mates** in early fall

28

Spider Map

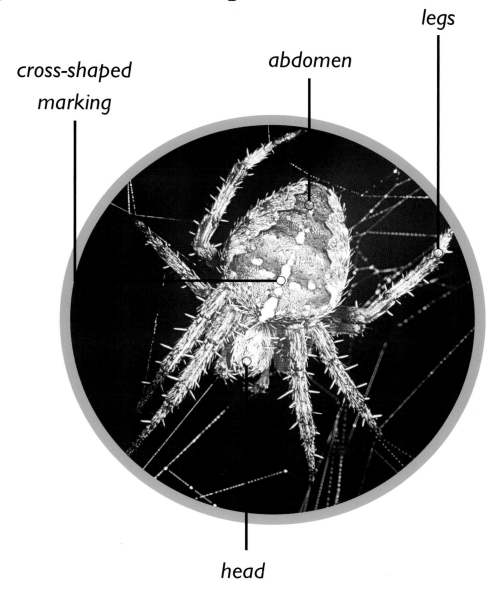

legs

abdomen

cross-shaped
marking

head

Glossary

ballooning flying on a silk thread blown by the wind

egg sac silk bag made by a female spider to hold her eggs

fangs sharp teeth that squeeze out poison

female girl animal

hatch break out of an egg

insects animals with six legs

male boy animal

mate when a male and female spider come together to make babies. It can also mean the partner an animal chooses to have babies with.

molting when the spider's old, tight skin falls off and a new, stretchy skin grows underneath it

poisonous filled with a bad-tasting or dangerous juice

silk strong, soft threads

spiderling baby spider

stems long stalks of plants

survive stay alive

swarm big group

web circle of silk that a spider spins

More Books to Read

Fridell, Ron, and Patricia Walsh. *Life Cycle of a Spider*. Chicago: Heinemann Library, 2001.

Ganeri, Anita. *Nature's Patterns: Animal Life Cycles*. Chicago: Heinemann Library, 2005.

Hartley, Karen, Chris Macro, and Philip Taylor. *Bug Books: Spiders*. Chicago: Heinemann Library, 1999.

Hughes, Monica. *Creepy Creatures: Spiders*. Chicago: Raintree, 2004.

Schwartz, David M. *Life Cycles: Jumping Spider*. Milwaukee: Gareth Stevens, 2001.

Watts, Barrie. *Watch It Grow: Spider*. Mankato, Minn.: Smart Apple Media, 2004.

Index